Book 2
Mind Benders®
Beginning

Deductive Thinking Skills

SERIES TITLES

Mind Benders® Beginning Book 1, Mind Benders® Beginning Book 2, Mind Benders® Warm Up, Mind Benders® A1, Mind Benders® A2, Mind Benders® A3, Mind Benders® A4, Mind Benders® B1, Mind Benders® B2, Mind Benders® B3, Mind Benders® B4, Mind Benders® C1, Mind Benders® C2, Mind Benders® C3

Michael Baker
Stephanie Stevens
Illustrated by Chanda Tsing

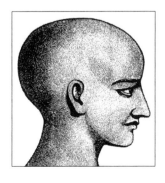
© 2005
THE CRITICAL THINKING CO.
(BRIGHT MINDS™)
www.CriticalThinking.com
P.O. Box 1610 • Seaside • CA 93955-1610
Phone 800-458-4849 • FAX 831-393-3277
ISBN 0-89455-873-0
Printed in the United States of America

TABLE OF CONTENTS

TEACHER SUGGESTIONS

PURPOSE

Beginning Mind Benders® help students develop comprehension, deductive reasoning, visual tracking, and fine motor skills. These logic activities can build confidence and improve self esteem.

MATERIALS

Use a pencil and have an eraser handy. The clues are challenging; understanding the chart usually takes a little practice.

BUILDING CONFIDENCE AND IMPROVING SELF-ESTEEM

This type of problem-solving is new to students. Praise students' success with every clue and discuss their determination to finish these challenging activities. My favorite expression to use with students is, "You are so smart." Try to instill in them the confidence to apply this problem-solving skill to other schoolwork. Help them to identify themselves as tenacious problem- solvers.

TEACHING SUGGESTIONS

When you first introduce students to Mind Benders®, work through the problems together until the students are confident enough to tackle the problems on their own. As you work through the problems, help them do the following:

1. Understand the chart
   a. Each person, animal, or object in the problem is represented on the chart. When you read the problem to the students, point to each item on the chart. When you read the first couple of clues, point to each item targeted in the clue.
   b. Each person, animal, or object in the chart has its own row or column. The intersection of each row and column is where the students indicate if the relationship is true or false (yes or no is often easier to understand). It may take some practice, but they usually get it after completing a few problems.
   c. Teach them to fill in as much information on the chart as they can after each clue. Children commonly begin by trying to solve the Mind Bender® without filling in all the "false" (no) relationships. This will work for some of the early problems, but, eventually, students will encounter more challenging problems. **Ask students to always mark all the true and false (yes and no) information learned from every clue.**

2. Help students with the clues in the beginning until they have some success and gain some confidence, then slowly challenge them to interpret the clues on their own. I frequently tell students that I know they can solve this clue because they have already solved harder clues. Knowing when to help and when to challenge can be difficult, but whether students succeed or become frustrated, praise their effort and their current and/or past success.

3. Pay special attention to the first few problems in each section. It is common for students to perform better in certain sections than in others, so don't be surprised if a student does well in the logic section but struggles in the math section. If a section becomes too frustrating for a student, move to another section. Return to the previous section once the student has had more practice and feels more confident; it is not necessary to go through the book sequentially.

4. In the Solutions section, the numbers on each chart indicate the clue(s) used to fill in that square.

5. Have fun! Remember to teach students that critical thinking is fun and reinforce that they are good at it.

HOW TO USE A CHART

A Mind Bender® problem gives you two lists of things and asks you to match each item in one list with an item in the other list by writing yes or no. In Activity 1, the student will match three people with their favorite way to travel. This activity is completed below as an example.

Example: Activity 1

A girl, a boy, and their mom have favorite ways to travel. Use the clues and chart to find each one's favorite way to travel.

     1. The mom's ride never leaves the ground.
     2. The boy's ride is the fastest.

Solution:

1. Read Clue 1. Look at each of the rides shown at the top of the chart. The boat cannot belong to the mom because it travels on water, nor can the jet because it travels in the air. The car must belong to the mom. Therefore, the car cannot belong to the boy or the girl.

2. Mark your answers on the chart. Draw Y for yes in the box under the under the car in the mom's row. Draw N for no in the other two boxes under the car and in the other two boxes in the Mom's row. Look at your chart: it shows the car belongs to the mom, not to the girl or boy.

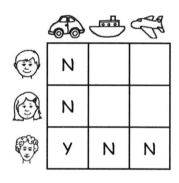

3. Read Clue 2. The boy's ride is the fastest. Is a jet faster than a boat? This clue tells us that the boy's ride is the jet.

4. Mark your answers on the chart. Draw Y for yes in the box under the jet in the boy's row. Draw N for no in the other empty box under the jet and in the other empty box in the boy's row. This means that the jet belongs to the boy, not to the girl.

N		N
N	N	Y
Y	N	N

5. Look at the chart. If the jet belongs to the boy and the car belongs to the mom, then the boat must belong to the girl. Draw Y for yes in the last empty box.

N	Y	N
N	N	Y
Y	N	N

ACTIVITY 1

DIRECTIONS: Fill in the chart using Y for yes or N for no as you solve the puzzle.

A girl, a boy, and their mom have favorite ways to travel. Find each person's favorite ride.

1. The mom's ride never leaves the ground.

2. The boy's ride is the fastest.

ACTIVITY 2

DIRECTIONS: Fill in the chart using Y for yes or N for no as you solve the puzzle.

A girl, a boy, and their uncle have their own horses. Find each person's horse.

1. The girl's horse and the boy's horse are all one color.

2. The boy's horse is the little sister of the uncle's horse.

ACTIVITY 3

DIRECTIONS: Fill in the chart using Y for yes or N for no as you solve the puzzle.

A girl, a boy, their mother, and their father have their own pet fish. Find each person's fish.

1. The girl's fish has more dots than the other fish.

2. The mom's fish has more dots than the dad's fish, but fewer dots than the boy's fish.

ACTIVITY 4

DIRECTIONS: Fill in the chart using Y for yes or N for no as you solve the puzzle.

Find each boy's first name.

1. The tallest boy is a friend of Bob and Ken.

2. Tom is shorter than the three other boys.

3. Bob is taller than Tom and Ken.

ACTIVITY 5

DIRECTIONS: Fill in the chart using Y for yes or N for no as you solve the puzzle.

Find each person's house.

1. The girl with straight hair lives in the house with the fewest windows.

2. The boy with a cap lives in a house with one more window than the curly-haired girl's house.

ACTIVITY 6

DIRECTIONS: Fill in the chart using Y for yes or N for no as you solve the puzzle.

Pam				
Dawn				
Rae				
Jan				

Pam, Dawn, Rae, and Jan are sisters. Find each girl's name.

1. Pam wears a cap and is taller than Rae and Jan.

2. Rae is shorter than Dawn, but taller than Jan.

ACTIVITY 7

DIRECTIONS: Fill in the chart using Y for yes or N for no as you solve the puzzle.

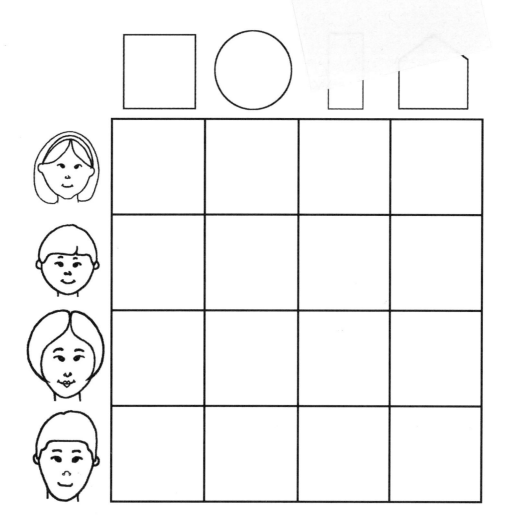

A girl, a boy, and their mom and dad all have favorite shapes. Find each person's favorite shape.

1. The dad's and the mom's shapes have sides of different lengths.

2. The girl's shape has no straight lines.

3. The boy's shape has one less side than the mom's shape.

ACTIVITY 8

DIRECTIONS: Fill in the chart using Y for yes or N for no as you solve the puzzle.

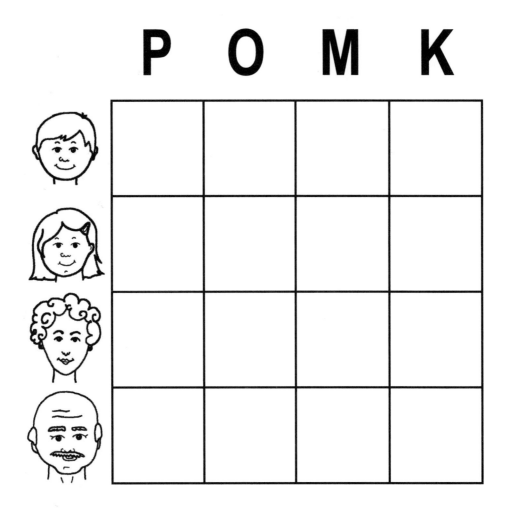

A boy, girl, their mom, and their grandfather have each picked one of the letters above. Find each person's chosen letter.

1. The grandfather's letter is made up of both straight lines and curves.

2. The mom's and girl's letters are made with only straight lines.

3. The mom's letter is the beginning sound in the word for "wet dirt."

ACTIVITY 9

DIRECTIONS: Fill in the chart using Y for yes or N for no as you solve the puzzle.

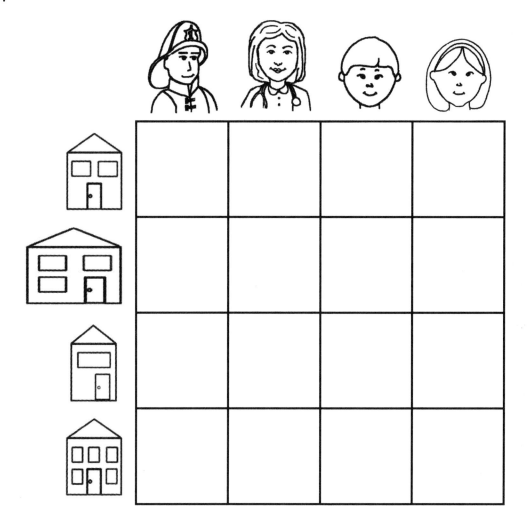

A fireman, doctor, boy, and girl all live in different houses. Find which house belongs to each person.

1. The girl's house has more than two windows and is not the widest.

2. The fireman's house has fewer than three windows.

3. The doctor's house has one more window than the fireman's and two more windows than the boy's.

ACTIVITY 10

DIRECTIONS: Fill in the chart using Y for yes or N for no as you solve the puzzle.

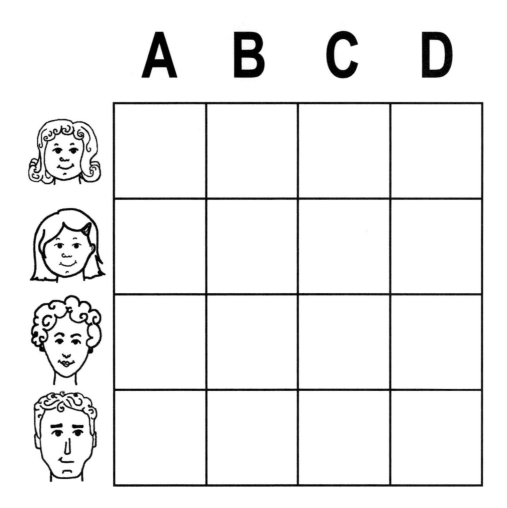

Two girls and their parents make up the Sanchez family. Find the first letter of each person's name.

1. People say Dona gets her curly hair from her father, Carlos.

2. Anita is younger than Bonita but older than Dona.

ACTIVITY 11

DIRECTIONS: Fill in the chart using Y for yes or N for no as you solve the puzzle.

Two students and two teachers have favorite fruits. Find each person's favorite fruit.

1. The name of the boy's favorite fruit has the most syllables, and Mr. Fox's has the fewest syllables.

2. Ms. Sharp's fruit grows larger than the girl's fruit.

ACTIVITY 12

DIRECTIONS: Fill in the chart using Y for yes or N for no as you solve the puzzle.

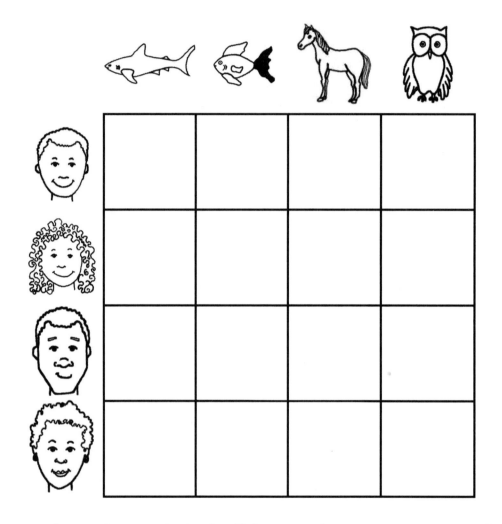

A boy, girl, mom, and dad all have their own pets. Find each person's pet.

1. The boy's pet has either wings or hooves.

2. The mom's pet cannot swim or fly.

3. The dad's pet is faster and bigger than the girl's pet.

ACTIVITY 13

DIRECTIONS: Fill in the chart using Y for yes or N for no as you solve the puzzle.

A mom, dad, grandmother, and grandfather all had dinner together. Find out what each person ate.

1. Grandfather has no teeth, so he had broth.

2. Dad liked his food so much he had a second bowl.

3. Grandmother never has the same thing two nights in a row, so tomorrow she will have a burger.

ACTIVITY 14

DIRECTIONS: Fill in the chart using Y for yes or N for no as you solve the puzzle.

A girl, boy, aunt, and uncle each has his or her own horse. Find each person's horse.

1. The boy's horse is not black and white.

2. The aunt's horse is one color and has a black tail.

3. The girl's horse has stripes or spots, but not both.

ACTIVITY 15

DIRECTIONS: Fill in the chart using Y for yes or N for no as you solve the puzzle.

Two girls and two boys all are different ages. Find each person's age.

1. The curly-haired boy is two years older than the curly-haired girl.

2. Both girls are younger than both boys.

ACTIVITY 16

DIRECTIONS: Fill in the chart using Y for yes or N for no as you solve the puzzle.

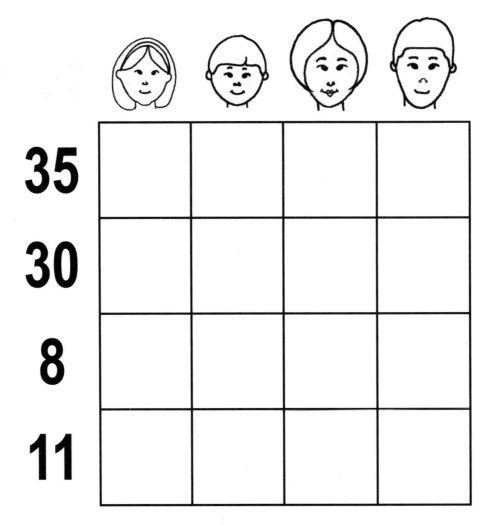

Find each person's age.

1. The dad will be forty before the mom.

2. The girl's birthday is in August, and the boy's birthday is in November.

3. The girl was at the boy's first birthday.

ACTIVITY 17

DIRECTIONS: Fill in the chart using Y for yes or N for no as you solve the puzzle.

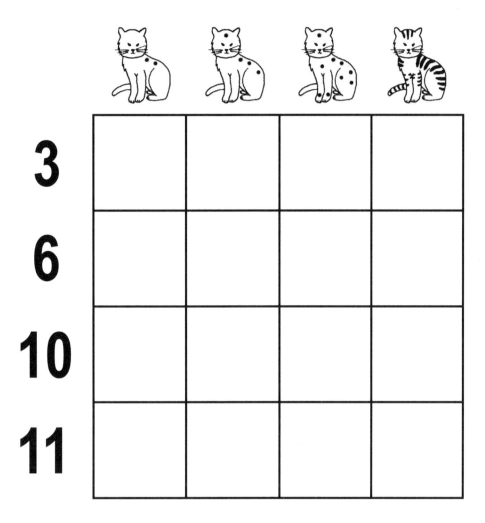

Find the age of each cat.

1. The youngest has seven fewer spots on the side you see than the oldest.

2. The striped cat and the oldest one are just a year apart.

ACTIVITY 18

DIRECTIONS: Fill in the chart using Y for yes or N for no as you solve the puzzle.

A boy, girl, mom, and dad each ate a different amount of candy. Match each person with the amount of candy he or she ate.

1. The mom ate less than the girl.

2. The girl ate less than the boy and less than the dad.

3. The boy ate five more than his sister.

ACTIVITY 19

DIRECTIONS: Fill in the chart using Y for yes or N for no as you solve the puzzle.

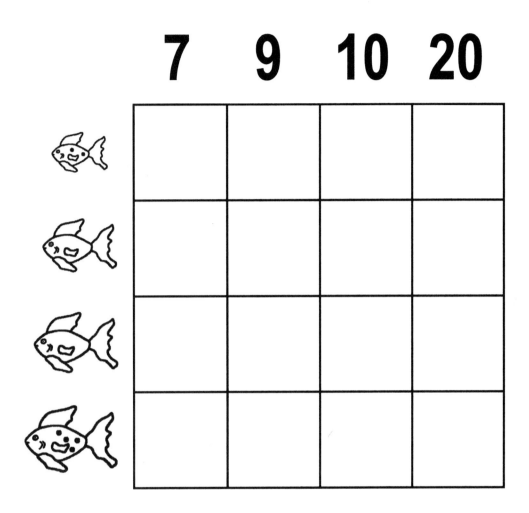

Find each fish's age.

1. The third oldest fish has no spots.

2. The youngest fish has spots and is smaller than the 9-year-old fish.

3. The oldest fish is bigger than the second oldest fish, who is bigger than the third oldest fish.

ACTIVITY 20

DIRECTIONS: Fill in the chart using Y for yes or N for no as you solve the puzzle.

A cat, snake, shark, and dog are all different ages. Find each animal's age.

1. The oldest does not have any legs.

2. The dog is four years older than the snake.

ACTIVITY 21

DIRECTIONS: Fill in the chart using Y for yes or N for no as you solve the puzzle.

Two boys and two girls played on a soccer team. Find out how many goals each person scored for his or her team.

1. The person with the fewest goals had to stop playing when she hurt her leg.

2. Dusty has the most curls and the most goals.

3. Tim has straighter hair but more goals than his friend Jack.

ACTIVITY 22

DIRECTIONS: Fill in the chart using Y for yes or N for no as you solve the puzzle.

A boy, girl, mom, and dad all arrived home at different times today. Find out when each person arrived home.

1. The mom arrived after her son and daughter.

2. The dad came home two hours after the boy.

ACTIVITY 23

DIRECTIONS: Fill in the chart using Y for yes or N for no as you solve the puzzle.

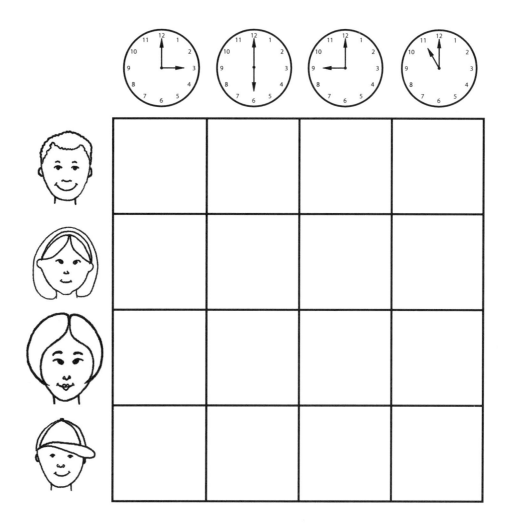

Three students and their teacher left their houses at different times. Find out when each person left his or her house.

1. The teacher left three hours after the girl and three hours before the boy with the cap.

ACTIVITY 24

DIRECTIONS: Fill in the chart using Y for yes or N for no as you solve the puzzle.

Four fish had fish for dinner. Find out how many fish each fish ate for dinner.

1. The black-tailed fish had more than the white fish.

2. The spotted fish had 5 more than the black-tailed fish.

ACTIVITY 25

DIRECTIONS: Fill in the chart using Y for yes or N for no as you solve the puzzle.

Two girls and two boys played on a basketball team. Find out how many points each person scored.

1. The curly-haired boy had more than fifteen points.

2. If Lee had made her last shot, she would have scored twelve points.

3. Tim scored fewer points than the curly-haired boy and girl.

ACTIVITY 26

DIRECTIONS: Fill in the chart using Y for yes or N for no as you solve the puzzle.

Two boys and two girls played baseball together. Find out how many runs each person scored.

1. The girls scored eleven runs together.

2. The boy with the cap had one less run than the girl with the necklace.

ACTIVITY 27

DIRECTIONS: Fill in the chart using Y for yes or N for no as you solve the puzzle.

The Rodriguez family had pizza for dinner. Find out how many pieces each family member had.

1. The boy had less than half a pizza and the mom had more than half a pizza.

2. The dad had one less piece than the mom.

ACTIVITY 28

DIRECTIONS: Fill in the chart using Y for yes or N for no as you solve the puzzle.

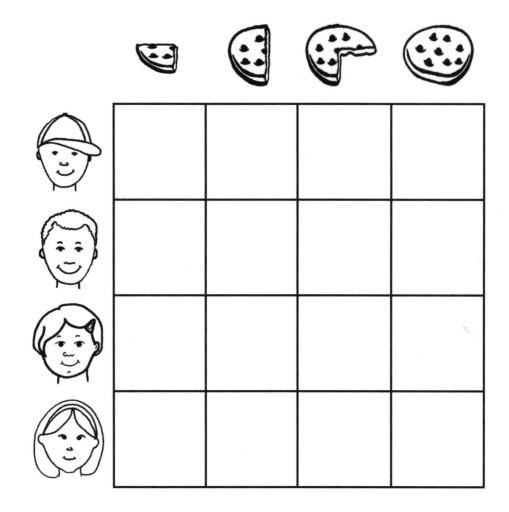

Two girls and two boys each received a cookie after lunch. Find out how much of his or her cookie each person ate.

1. The boy with a cap ate less cookie than either of the girls and half of what Zack ate.

2. The girl with the longer hair ate twice as much as Zack.

ACTIVITY 29

DIRECTIONS: Fill in the chart using Y for yes or N for no as you solve the puzzle.

	Donna	Tio	Anita	Rico

Find each person's name.

1. Donna is older than Tio and Anita, but younger than Rico.

ACTIVITY 30

DIRECTIONS: Fill in the chart using Y for yes or N for no as you solve the puzzle.

	seven	six	ten	twelve

A daughter, son, dad, and mom all saved dollars to spend at the store. Find out how many dollars each person saved.

1. If you add the dad's and the daughter's savings, you get twenty-two.

2. The mom tried to save seven dollars, but "fell short."

3. The girl ended up with "net" spelled backwards.

ACTIVITY 31

DIRECTIONS: Fill in the chart using Y for yes or N for no as you solve the puzzle.

	Bill	Jill	Ron	Don

Find each person's name.

1. Ron and Don will not wear white caps.

2. If Bill wears a cap, so will Ron.

ACTIVITY 32

DIRECTIONS: Fill in the chart using Y for yes or N for no as you solve the puzzle.

	Mark	Debbie	Teresa	Bradley

Find each person's name.

1. The curly-haired girl with the necklace has the most syllables in her name.

2. The curly-haired boy has the fewest syllables in his name.

ACTIVITY 33

DIRECTIONS: Fill in the chart using Y for yes or N for no as you solve the puzzle.

	cat	dog	bug	rat

Find each person's pet.

1. The names of the woman's pet and the boy's pet rhyme.

2. The name of the man's pet rhymes with "jug."

3. The name of woman's pet rhymes with "bat," "hat," and "cat."

ACTIVITY 34

DIRECTIONS: Fill in the chart using Y for yes or N for no as you solve the puzzle.

Find each person's name.

1. One of the people with curly hair has the letters "e" and "b" in her name.

2. The boy with curly hair was named for the month he was born.

ACTIVITY 35

DIRECTIONS: Fill in the chart using Y for yes or N for no as you solve the puzzle.

	yellow	red	black	silver

Each family member has a different favorite color. Figure out each person's favorite color.

1. Jack likes the color that rhymes with his name.

2. Jack's dad likes a color that rhymes with "fellow."

3. The daughter's second favorite color rhymes with "bed."

ACTIVITY 36

DIRECTIONS: Fill in the chart using Y for yes or N for no as you solve the puzzle.

	cold	cool	warm	hot
🧢				
👩				
🧑				
👧				

Each person likes his or her chocolate milk at a different temperature. Find each person's favorite temperature.

1. The woman and the boy always heat their milk.

2. The woman does not like her food or her drinks hot.

3. The boy likes his milk warmer than the man likes his milk and much warmer than the girl likes her milk

ACTIVITY 37

DIRECTIONS: Fill in the chart using Y for yes or N for no as you solve the puzzle.

	basketball	football	tennis	soccer
(curly hair girl)				
(boy)				
(curly hair boy)				
(girl)				

Find each person's sport.

1. You can't see Tom's curly hair under his helmet.

2. The soccer player's brother is the tennis player.

3. The girl with the necklace will play only basketball.

ACTIVITY 38

DIRECTIONS: Fill in the chart using Y for yes or N for no as you solve the puzzle.

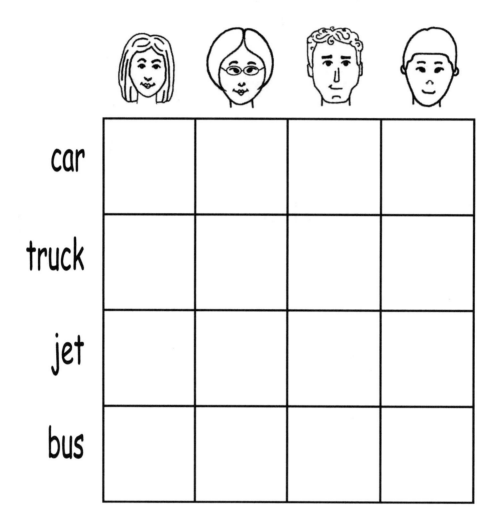

Find out what each person drives at work.

1. The truck driver misses her family on long trips.

2. The person with the glasses spends the least amount of time on the ground.

3. The curly-haired man drives a car to work, but not during his work.

ACTIVITY 39

DIRECTIONS: Fill in the chart using Y for yes or N for no as you solve the puzzle.

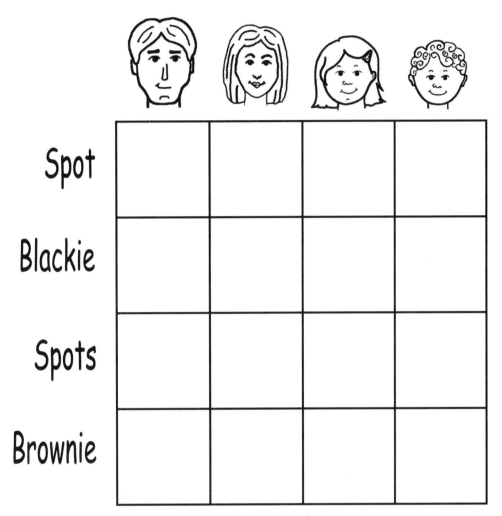

Each person's horse is named after the way the animal looks. Find the name of each person's horse.

1. The man's and the woman's horses are all one color.

2. Blackie's owner fell off and hit his head.

3. The boy's horse has a spot on his leg and his neck.

ACTIVITY 40

DIRECTIONS: Fill in the chart using Y for yes or N for no as you solve the puzzle.

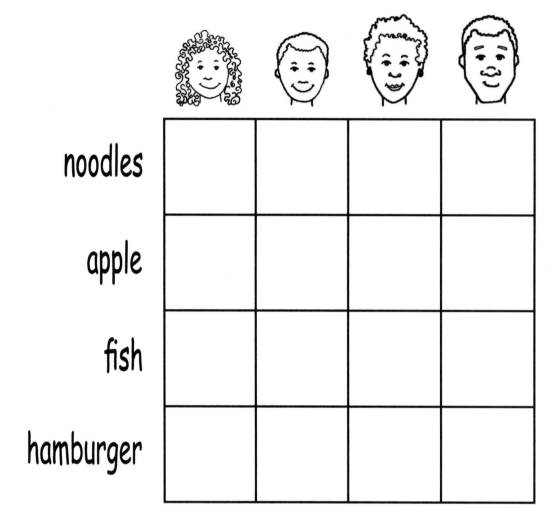

Find what each person ate for lunch.

1. The girl's food is not made from ham. It is made from beef.

2. The mom's food came off a tree.

3. The boy caught his food in his dad's boat.

ACTIVITY 41

DIRECTIONS: Fill in the chart using Y for yes or N for no as you solve the puzzle.

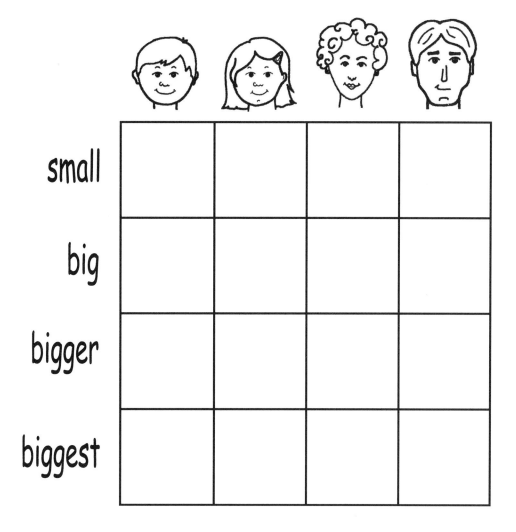

Each member of the Wilson Family picked an apple from a tree. Find out the size of apple each person picked.

1. The boy's apple was bigger than the girl's, but smaller than his mom's.

2. The girl's apple was bigger than her dad's, but not the biggest.

ACTIVITY 42

DIRECTIONS: Fill in the chart using Y for yes or N for no as you solve the puzzle.

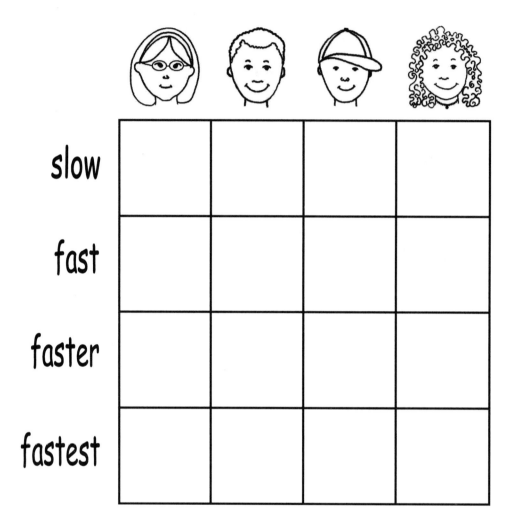

Four runners run a race. Find out how fast each person runs.

1. The boy with the cap runs ahead of the girl with the necklace, but behind the other boy.

2. The girl with the glasses has never lost to either of the boys.

1.

	🚗	⛴	✈
👧	N₁	Y₂	N₂
👦	N₁	N₂	Y₂
🧑‍🦱	Y₁	N₁	N₁

Clue 1 states that the mom's favorite ride never leaves the ground, so the mom's favorite is the car, since it never leaves the ground. Clue 2 says the boy's favorite is the fastest. The boy prefers the jet, since it is faster than the boat or the car. This leaves the boat as the girl's choice.

2.

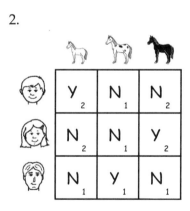

	🐎	🐎	🐎
👦	Y₂	N₁	N₂
👧	N₂	N₁	Y₂
🧑	N₁	Y₁	N₁

Since Clue 1 states that the boy and the girl have horses of one color, which means that the spotted horse belongs to their uncle. Clue 2 states that the boy's horse is the little sister of the uncle's horse, so the small, white horse belongs to the boy and the black horse belongs to the girl.

3.

	🐟	🐟	🐟	🐟
👦	N₂	N₂	Y₂	N₁
👩‍🦱	N₁	N₁	N₁	Y₁
🧑	Y₂	N₂	N₂	N₁
🧑‍🦱	N₂	Y₂	N₂	N₁

Based on Clue 1, the girl's fish is the one on the far right with 4 dots since it has more dots than the other fish. Clue 2 says that the mom's fish has more dots than the dad's but fewer than the boy's. This means that the mom's fish must be the one with 2 dots, the dad's fish is the one with 1 dot, and the boy's fish has to be the one with 3 dots.

4.

	🧍	🧍	🧍	🧍
Tom	Y₂	N₂	N₂	N₂
Bob	N₂	N₃	Y₃	N₁
Bill	N₂	N₂	N₂	Y₂
Ken	N₂	Y₃	N₃	N₁

Clue 1 states that the tallest boy is a friend of Bob and Ken, which means he is not either of those names. Clue 2 states that Tom is shorter than the 3 other boys, so he is the shortest boy on the far left. Both clues together mean that the name of the tallest boy is Bill. Clue 3 states that Bob is taller than Tom and Ken. So, with two boys shorter than him, Bob is the third from the left and Ken is the second from the left.

5.

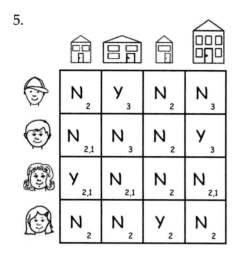

(boy with cap)	N 2	Y 3	N 2	N 3
(boy)	N 2,1	N 3	N 2	Y 3
(curly girl)	Y 2,1	N 2,1	N 2	N 2,1
(straight girl)	N 2	N 2	Y 2	N 2

Clue 1 states that the girl with the straight hair lives in the house with the fewest windows, the 1-window house. Clue 2 states that the boy wearing a cap lives in the house with one more window than that of the curly-haired girl's house. So, he lives in the 3-window house and the curly-haired girl lives in the 2-window house. Lastly, the boy not wearing a cap lives in the 5-window house.

6.

Pam	N 1	N 1	Y 1	N 1
Dawn	N 1	N 1	N 1	Y 2
Rae	N 2	Y 2	N 1	N 2
Jan	Y 2	N 2	N 1	N 2

Clue 1 states that Pam wears a cap and is taller than Rae and Jan. Only one girl has a cap, which means she is Pam. She's also taller than two of the girls, which means that Rae and Jan are the two girls on the left. Clue 2 states that Rae is shorter than Dawn, but taller than Jan. So, Jan is on the far left, Rae is second from the left, and Dawn is on the far right.

7.

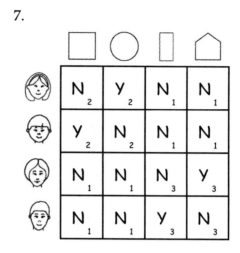

(mom)	N 2	Y 2	N 1	N 1
(dad)	Y 2	N 2	N 1	N 1
(girl)	N 1	N 1	N 3	Y 3
(boy)	N 1	N 1	Y 3	N 3

Based on clue 1, the dad's shape and the mom's shape are the rectangle and the pentagon, which have different lengths. So the girl and boy have the circle and the square. Clue 2 states that the girl's shape has no straight lines, so it is the circle and the boy's shape is the square. Clue 3 states that the boy's shape has one less side than the mom's, so the mom must have the pentagon and the dad has the rectangle.

8.

	P	O	M	K
(boy)	N 1	Y 2	N 2	N 2
(girl)	N 1	N 2	N 3	Y 3
(curly man)	N 1	N 2	Y 3	N 3
(mustache man)	Y 1	N 1	N 1	N 1

Clue 1 states that the grandfather's letter has both straight lines and curves, so it isn't M, K, or O. It has to be P. Clue 2 states that the mom's and girl's letters have only straight lines, so they're either M or K. That means that the boy's letter is O. Clue 3 states that the mom's letter is the first sound in "wet dirt," which is "mud." So, mom's letter is M, which leaves the K as the girl's letter.

9.

	👮	👩‍⚕️	👦	👧
🏠	Y 3	N 3	N 3	N 1
🏠	N 2	Y 3	N 3	N 1
🏠	N 3	N 3	Y 3	N 1
🏠	N 1	N 1	N 1	Y 1

Clue 1 states that the girl's house has more than two windows and is not the widest. The girl's house is the 5-window house. Clue 2 states that the fireman's house has fewer than three windows, so it is either the 1- or 2-window house. Finally, Clue 3 states that the doctor's house has one more window than the fireman's and two more windows than the boy's. So, the 2-window house is the fireman's, while the 3-window house belongs to the doctor. The 1-window house is the boy's.

10.

	A	B	C	D
👩‍🦱	N 1	N 1	N 1	Y 1
👩	Y 2	N 2	N 1	N 1
👦‍🦱	N 2	Y 2	N 1	N 1
👨	N 1	N 1	Y 1	N 1

Clue 1 states that Dona has curly hair like her father, Carlos. The father's name begins with C, Carlos, and the curly-haired girl is Dona, which begins with D. Clue 2 states that Anita is younger than Bonita and older than Dona, so Bonita is the mother's name. Anita is the girl with straight hair.

11.

	🍌	🍎	🍒	🍇
👦	Y 1	N 1	N 1	N 1
👧	N 1	N 3	Y 3	N 2
👩‍🦱	N 1	Y 3	N 3	N 2
👨	N 1	N 2	N 2	Y 2

Clue 1 states that the name of the boy's favorite fruit has the most syllables. "Banana" has 3 syllables, more than the other fruit, so that's the boy's favorite. Clue 2 states that Mr. Fox's favorite fruit has the fewest syllables, so his would be the grapes. Clue 3 says that Ms. Sharp's fruit grows larger than the girl's, and an apple grows larger than a cherry. So, Ms. Sharp's favorite fruit is the apple and the girl's is the cherry.

12.

	🦈	🐟	🐴	🦉
👦	N 1	N 1	N 2	Y 2
👩‍🦱	N 3	Y 3	N 2	N 2
👨	Y 3	N 3	N 2	N 2
👦‍🦱	N 2	N 2	Y 2	N 2

Based on Clue 1, the boy's pet has either wings or hooves, so it isn't either fish. Clue 2 states that the mom's pet cannot swim or fly, so her pet is the horse. This means the boy's pet is the owl. Clue 3 says the dad's pet is faster and bigger than the girl's pet. The shark is both faster and bigger, so it belongs to the dad. The girl's pet is the fish.

13.

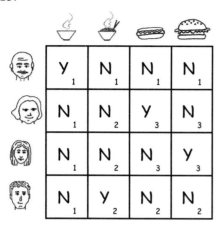

	🍲	🍜	🌭	🍔
😊	Y 1	N 1	N 1	N 1
😊	N 1	N 2	Y 3	N 3
😊	N 1	N 2	N 3	Y 3
😊	N 1	Y 2	N 2	N 2

Clue 1 states that the grandfather has no teeth, so he had broth. The only food that could be broth is in the first bowl. Clue 2 states that Dad has a second bowl of food. The only other bowl is the second from the left, which must be his. Based on Clue 3, Grandmother never has the same thing two nights in a row. Since tomorrow she'll have a burger, that means today she had a hot dog. That leaves the hamburger for the mom.

14.

	👧	👦	👩	👨
🐴	N 2	Y 2	N 2	N 2
🐴	Y 3	N 1	N 2	N 3
🦓	N 3	N 1	N 2	Y 3
🐴	N 2	N 2	Y 2	N 2

Clue 1 states that the boy's horse is not black and white, so it is not a spotted horse. Clue 2 states that the aunt's horse is one color and has a black tail, so hers must be the black horse. That means that the boy's is the white horse. Clue 3 states that the girl's horse has stripes or spots, but not both. So, hers is the second horse down and the uncle's is the one with both stripes and spots.

15.

	6	**7**	**8**	**10**
👦	N 2	N 2	N 2	Y 2
👦	N 2	N 1	Y 2	N 2
👧	N 2	Y 2	N 2	N 2
👧	Y 2	N 1	N 2	N 2

Clue 1 states that the curly-haired boy is two years older than the curly-haired girl. They could be either 6 and 8, or 8 and 10. Clue 2 states that both girls are younger than both boys, which means that the girls are 6 and 7. Since the curly-haired boy is 2 years older than the curly-haired girl, that means that the curly-haired girl is 6 and the curly-haired boy is 8. The straight-haired girl is 7, and the straight-haired boy is 10.

16.

	👧	👦	👩	👨
35	N 1	N 1	N 1	Y 1
30	N 1	N 1	Y 1	N 1
8	N 3	Y 3	N 1	N 1
11	Y 3	N 3	N 1	N 1

Based on Clue 1, Dad will be 40 before the mom, so he is older than her and is 35. The mom is 30. Clue 2 tells the month of the girl's and boy's birthdays, a fact that doesn't matter in the problem. Clue 3 states that the girl was at the boy's first birthday, which means she's at least one year older than him. The girl is 11 and the boy is 8.

17.

	🐱	🐱	🐱	🐱
3	Y₁	N₁	N₁	N₁
6	N₁	Y₂	N₁	N₂
10	N₁	N₂	N₁	Y₂
11	N₁	N₁	Y₁	N₁

Clue 1 states that the youngest cat has seven fewer spots than the oldest cat. The youngest is the cat with two spots and is three years old. The oldest cat, with 9 spots, is eleven years old. Clue 2 states that the striped cat and the oldest cat are one year apart, so the striped cat is ten years old. That means that the cat with four spots is six years old.

18.

	😀	😀	😀	😀
10	N₂	N₁	N₂	Y₂
20	N₂	Y₂	N₂	N₂
25	Y₃	N₂	N₃	N₂
29	N₃	N₂	Y₃	N₁

Clue 1 states that the mom ate less candy than the girl. Clue 2 states that the girl ate less than either the boy or the dad. These two clues together mean that the mom ate the least candy, ten pieces, and the girl ate 20 pieces. Clue 3 says that the boy ate five more pieces than the girl, so he ate 25 pieces and the dad ate 29.

19.

	7	**9**	**10**	**20**
🐟	Y₂	N₁	N₂	N₂
🐟	N₂	Y₃	N₃	N₃
🐟	N₂	N₃	Y₃	N₃
🐟	N₂	N₁	N₃	Y₃

Based on Clue 1, the third oldest fish (9) has no spots, so it is not the smallest nor the biggest. Clue 2 states that the youngest fish (7) has spots and is smaller than the 9-year-old fish, so it is the smallest fish. Clue 3 states that the oldest fish (20) is bigger than either the second oldest fish or the third oldest fish, so it is the biggest fish. Then the second oldest fish (10) is the second biggest fish and the third oldest fish (9) is the third biggest fish.

20.

	🐱	🐍	🦈	🐕
11	N₁	N₂	Y₂	N₁
9	Y₂	N₂	N₂	N₂
6	N₂	N₂	N₂	Y₂
2	N₂	Y₂	N₂	N₂

Clue 1 says the oldest animal has no legs. That could be either the snake or the shark. Clue 2 states that the dog is four years older than the snake, which makes the dog 6 and the snake 2. Since the oldest has no legs, it has to be the shark. That leaves the cat at age 9.

21.

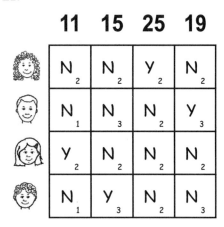

Clue 1 states that the person with the fewest goals stopped playing when *she* hurt her leg, so a girl had the fewest goals. Clue 2 states that Dusty has the most curls and the most goals, so the curly-haired girl is Dusty with 25 goals. That means the straight-haired girl scored 11 goals. Clue 3 states that Tim has straighter hair but more goals than his friend Jack. That means that Tim is the short-haired boy with 19 goals, and the other boy is Jack.

22.

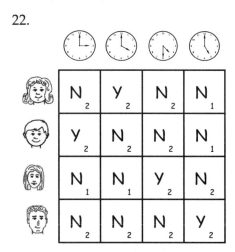

In Clue 1, the mom came home after her son and daughter, so she was not the first or second earliest (3:00 or 4:00) and they were not the latest (5:00). Clue 2 states that the dad came home two hours after the boy, so the dad came home at 5:00 and the boy came home at 3:00. Since the mother came after the boy and girl, she came home at 4:30 and her daughter came home at 4:00.

23.

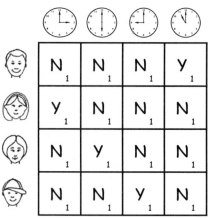

There's only one clue here, and it states that the teacher left home three hours after the girl and three hours before the boy with the cap. This means that there must be six hours between the girl's time and the capped boy's time, and the time exactly in between them must be the teacher's time. Therefore, the teacher left at 6:00, the girl at 3:00, the capped boy at 9:00, and the other boy at 11:00.

24.

	10	20	25	35
	N₁	Y₂	N₂	N₂
	N₂	N₂	Y₂	N₂
	Y₂	N₂	N₂	N₁
	N₂	N₂	N₂	Y₂

Clue 1 states that the black-tailed fish had more than the white fish, so it didn't eat the fewest and the white fish didn't eat the most. Clue 2 states that the spotted fish had 5 more than the black-tailed fish, which means that the spotted fish had 25 and the black-tailed fish had 20. So, the white fish had 10 and the striped fish had 35.

25.

10   12   25   15

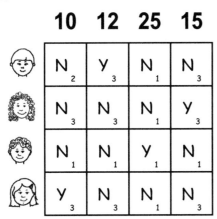

	10	12	25	15
(face 1)	N 2	Y 3	N 1	N 3
(face 2)	N 3	N 3	N 1	Y 3
(face 3)	N 1	N 1	Y 1	N 1
(face 4)	Y 3	N 3	N 1	N 3

Clue 1 states that the curly-haired boy had more than fifteen points, so he had 25. In Clue 2, if Lee had made her last shot, *she* would have scored twelve points, which means that Lee is one of the two girls. Since the clue says "if," that means she didn't make her last shot and only scored 10. Clue 3 states that Tim scored fewer points than the curly-haired boy and girl. Since Lee scored 10, Tim scored 12 points and the curly-haired girl scored 15. So, Lee is the straight-haired girl.

26.

4   6   7   10

	4	6	7	10
(face 1)	N 2	N 1	Y 2	N 1
(face 2)	N 1	Y 2	N 1	N 2
(face 3)	Y 2	N 1	N 2	N 1
(face 4)	N 1	N 2	N 1	Y 2

Clue 1 stated that the total of the girls' scores comes to 11. The two numbers that total 11 are 7 & 4, so those are the girl's scores. Clue 2 states that the boy with the cap had one less run than the curly-haired girl. The only numbers that are one number apart are 6 and 7, so the capped boy scored 6 and the curly-haired girl scored 7. That makes the other girl's score 4 and the other boy's score 10.

27.

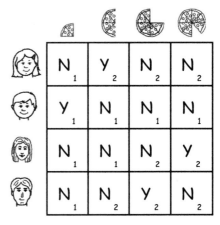

	(pizza)	(pizza)	(pizza)	(pizza)
(face 1)	N 1	Y 2	N 2	N 2
(face 2)	Y 1	N 1	N 1	N 1
(face 3)	N 1	N 1	N 2	Y 2
(face 4)	N 1	N 2	Y 2	N 2

Based on Clue 1, the boy had less than half a pizza. Half a pizza is 4 pieces, so he had 2 pieces. The mom had more than half a pizza, so she could have had either 6 or 7 pieces. In Clue 2, if the dad has one less piece than the mom, then he had 6 and she had 7. So, the girl had 4 pieces.

28.

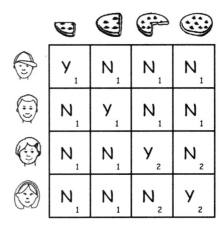

	(cookie)	(cookie)	(cookie)	(cookie)
(face 1)	Y 1	N 1	N 1	N 1
(face 2)	N 1	Y 1	N 1	N 1
(face 3)	N 1	N 1	Y 2	N 2
(face 4)	N 1	N 1	N 2	Y 2

Clue 1 states that the boy with the cap ate less cookie than either of the girls and half of what Zack ate, so he ate the smallest piece: a fourth of a cookie. Since the capped boy ate half of what Zack ate, then Zack ate half a cookie. Based on Clue 2, the longer-haired girl ate the whole cookie, leaving the short-haired girl chomping down on the remaining cookie piece: three-quarters of a cookie.

29.

	Donna	Tio	Anita	Rico
(boy)	N 1	Y 1	N 1	N 1
(woman)	N 1	N 1	Y 1	N 1
(man)	N 1	N 1	N 1	Y 1
(girl)	Y 1	N 1	N 1	N 1

There is only one clue, and it states that Donna is older than Tio and Anita, but younger than Rico. This means that Donna is the mom and Rico is the father. Anita and Tio are the kids.

30.

	seven	six	ten	twelve
(girl)	N 1	N 1	Y 3	N 3
(boy)	Y 2	N 2	N 1	N 1
(man)	N 1	N 1	N 3	Y 3
(woman)	N 2	Y 2	N 1	N 1

Based on Clue 1, if the dad's and the daughter's savings are added together, they make $22. Checking number combinations, only $10 and $12 equal $22, so those are the savings of the dad and daughter. Then the mom and son had savings of $7 or $6. Clue 2 states that the mom tried to save $7 but "fell short," so she saved $6 and the son saved $7. Clue 3 states the girl's savings is spelled "net" backwards, which is "ten" or $10. That means that the father saved $12.

31.

	Bill	Jill	Ron	Don
(boy, white cap)	N 1	N 1	N 2	Y 2
(boy, black cap)	N 1	N 1	Y 2	N 2
(boy, cap)	Y 1	N 1	N 1	N 1
(girl)	N 1	Y 1	N 1	N 1

The only girl is Jill. Clue 1 states that Ron and Don don't wear white caps. So, the boy with the white cap must be Bill. Clue 2 says that when Bill wears a cap, so does Ron. Ron wears the black cap. Don wears no cap at all.

32.

	Mark	Debbie	Teresa	Bradley
(girl)	N 1	Y 1	N 1	N 1
(curly boy)	Y 2	N 1	N 1	N 2
(curly girl)	N 1	N 1	Y 1	N 1
(boy)	N 2	N 1	N 1	Y 2

Clue 1 states that the curly-haired girl with the necklace has the most syllables in her name, so she would be Teresa (3 syllables). So, the other girl must be Debbie. Clue 2 states that the curly-haired boy has the fewest syllables in his name, so he would be Mark. That makes Bradley the other boy.

33.

	cat	dog	bug	rat
	Y 3	N 1	N 1	N 3
	N 1	Y 2	N 2	N 1
	N 3	N 1	N 1	Y 3
	N 1	N 2	Y 2	N 1

Clue 1 states that the names of the woman's pet and the boy's pet rhyme. Their pets are the cat and the rat. Since clue 2 says the name of the man's pet rhymes with "jug," his pet is the bug. That means the dog is the girl's pet. Based on Clue 3, the woman's pet is not the cat, so it is the rat. The cat is the boy's pet.

34.

Jill	N 1	N 1	Y 1	N 1
Deb	N 1	N 1	N 1	Y 1
Ben	N 2	Y 2	N 1	N 1
August	Y 2	N 2	N 1	N 1

Based on Clue 1, one person with curly hair has the letters "e" and "b" in *her* name. This means the curly-haired girl is Deb. Since there's only one other girl and one other girl's name, the other girl is Jill. Clue 2 states that the boy with curly hair was named for the month he was born. August is the only month listed as a name, so the curly-haired boy is August. That leaves Ben as the name of the straight-haired boy.

35.

	yellow	red	black	silver
	N 2	N 3	N 1	Y 3
	N 1	N 1	Y 1	N 1
	Y 2	N 2	N 1	N 2
	N 2	Y 3	N 1	N 3

Clue 1 states that Jack likes the color that rhymes with his name, so his glass is black. Clue 2 states that the dad likes the one that rhymes with "fellow," so his is yellow. Clue 3 states the daughter's second favorite color rhymes with "bed," which is red. So silver is the girl's favorite and the mother's is red.

36.

	cold	cool	warm	hot
	N 1	N 1	N 2	Y 2
	Y 3	N 3	N 1	N 1
	N 3	Y 3	N 1	N 1
	N 1	N 1	Y 2	N 2

Clue 1 states that the woman and boy always heat their milk, so they do not drink it cold or cool. Clue 2 says that the woman does not like her food or her drinks hot, so she must like hers warm. Then the boy likes his milk hot. Clue 3 states the boy likes his milk warmer than the man likes his and much warmer than the girl likes hers. So, the man's milk is cool, and the girl's milk is cold.

37.

	basketball	football	tennis	soccer
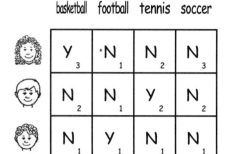	Y 3	N 1	N 2	N 3
	N 2	N 1	Y 2	N 2
	N 1	Y 1	N 1	N 1
	N 3	N 1	N 2	Y 3

Based on information in Clue 1, Tom has curly hair and wears a helmet, which is worn in football. Clue 2 states the soccer player's brother is the tennis player, so the second boy plays tennis, and the soccer player is a girl. Clue 3 states that the girl with the necklace plays only basketball, so the soccer player is the other girl.

38.

car	N 2	N 2	N 3	Y 3
truck	Y 2	N 2	N 1	N 1
jet	N 2	Y 2	N 2	N 2
bus	N 2	N 2	Y 3	N 3

Based on Clue 1, the truck driver is a woman. Clue 2 states that the person wearing glasses spends the least amount of time on the ground. So, the woman in glasses pilots the jet. Then the other woman is the truck driver. Clue 3 states the curly-haired man drives a car *to* work, but not during work. That means he drives the bus, while the other man drives a car at work.

39.

Spot	N 1	N 1	Y 3	N 3
Blackie	Y 2	N 2	N 1	N 1
Spots	N 1	N 1	N 3	Y 3
Brownie	N 2	Y 2	N 1	N 1

Based on Clue 1, the horses named Blackie and Brownie belong to the man and the woman, since they're each only one color. Clue 2 says that Blackie's owner hit *his* head, which means that the man's horse is Blackie, so the woman's is Brownie. Clue 3 says that the boy's horse has more than one spot, so his name would be Spots. That means the girl owns the horse named Spot.

40.

noodles	N 1	N 3	N 2	Y 3
apple	N 1	N 2	Y 2	N 2
fish	N 1	Y 3	N 2	N 3
hamburger	Y 1	N 1	N 1	N 1

Based on Clue 1, the girl's food includes beef, so it's a hamburger. Clue 2 states the mom's food came off a tree, so her lunch is the apple. Clue 3 says that the boy caught his food in a boat, so his is the fish. What's left? Noodles for dad.

41.

small	N 1	N 2	N 1	Y 2,1
big	N 2,1	Y 2,1	N 2,1	N 2,1
bigger	Y 2,1	N 2,1	N 2,1	N 2
biggest	N 1	N 1	Y 2,1	N 2

Based on Clue 1, neither the boy nor the girl has the biggest apple, and the boy and his mom don't have the small apple. In Clue 2, the girl's apple is bigger than her dad's. This means the dad cannot have the biggest or the bigger apple and the girl cannot have the smallest apple. Using both clues, the dad must have the small apple and the mom the biggest. Therefore, the girl's apple is big and the boy's bigger.

42.

slow	N 2,1	N 1	N 1	Y 2,1
fast	N 2,1	N 2,1	Y 2,1	N 2,1
faster	N 2,1	Y 2,1	N 2,1	N 2,1
fastest	Y 2,1	N 2,1	N 1	N 1

Based on Clue 1, neither the capped boy nor the other boy is the slow runner. Clue 2 states the girl wearing glasses has never lost to either of the boys. Based on both clues, the girl with the glasses is the fastest, the capped boy is fast, and the other boy is faster. The slow runner is the curly-haired girl with the necklace.

Look at each pair of pictures.
There's always two of a kind.
Find how each pair is alike.
Then you'll know what to find.

For additional information about this product or other Critical Thinking products,
call 800-458-4849 or visit www.CriticalThinking.com.

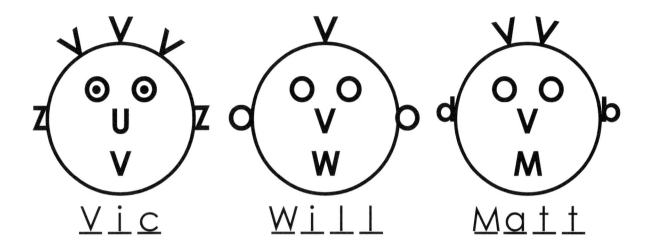

1. Look at each face above, then find its unfinished picture below. Use a pencil to draw in all the missing parts.

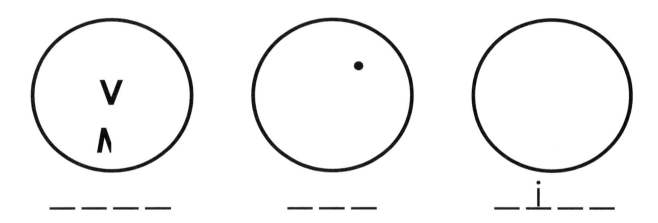

2. Color the faces that have the most "V"s using one color.

3. Color the faces that have the most "O"s using three colors.

4. Color the faces that have an "M" using two colors.

For additional information about this product or other Critical Thinking products, call 800-458-4849 or visit www.CriticalThinking.com.

ZEBRA

I live in Africa. My stripes make a beautiful pattern.

Draw the missing parts of the picture, then color the picture. Can you draw trees to give me shade? Can you add something else to the picture?

For additional information about this product or other Critical Thinking products, call 800-458-4849 or visit www.CriticalThinking.com.

This is Braden on his birthday three years ago.

1.　How old was he then? _____

2.　How old is Braden now? _____

3.　Draw the candles on his cake below.

For additional information about this product or other Critical Thinking products,
call 800-458-4849 or visit www.CriticalThinking.com.

1.  begins with f. begins with s.

Write the beginning letter for each object below.

_____   _____   _____   _____

2.  begins with p. begins with b.

Write the beginning letter for each object below.

_____   _____   _____   _____

3.  begins with w.  begins with r.

Write the beginning letter for each object below.

_____   _____   _____   _____

I'm a tasty fruit,
And I rhyme with glum;
And once I was stuck,
To Jack Horner's thumb.

What am I? ....

To the dump I haul,
The garbage of the city;
And I rhyme with duck,
I hope you like this ditty.

What am I? ....

I start with an 'S',
And end with 'P';
And sail upon,
The salty sea.

What am I? ....

For additional information about this product or other Critical Thinking products,
call 800-458-4849 or visit www.CriticalThinking.com.